P9-DDG-534

100 ways to teach your child about God

100 ways to teach your child about God

BY KARYN HENLEY

Tyndale House Publishers, Inc.
Wheaton, Illinois

TYNDALE
KIDS

Edited by Betty Free

Designed by Julie Chen

Library of Congress Cataloging-in-Publication Data

Henley, Karyn.
  100 ways to teach your child about God / Karyn Henley.
    p. cm.
  ISBN 0-8423-3784-9 (SC)
  1. Christian education of children. 2. Christian education—Home training. 3. God—Attributes—Study and teaching.
I. Title: One hundred ways to teach your child about God. II. Title.
BV1590.H46 2000
248.845—dc21
                                  00-022190

Printed in Singapore

06 05 04 03 02
7   6   5   4   3

contents

introduction

The Farmer

JESUS once told a story about a farmer who planted seeds. Some seeds fell on the hard path where birds ate them. Some seeds fell on rocky soil, where they grew quickly. But the heat of the sun soon withered the plants because their root systems were shallow. Some seeds fell among thorns. As the new plants grew, they were choked out. But the seeds that fell onto soft, fertile soil thrived and grew and produced a great harvest (Matthew 13:1-23).

IN a very real way, we are seed planters. God's message is the seed. Hearts are the soil. Sometimes the message doesn't even sink in. Perhaps it's because the heart is hard and beaten down. Or perhaps the message has not been communi-cated in a way that is understandable. Either way, the evil one is able to snatch the seed away easily.

SOMETIMES it appears that God's message has been received readily and is growing quickly. But the roots have not gone very deep. When troubles come, it's as if this person never knew God at all.

OTHER people receive God's message and begin to grow. But the worries of life and dependence on our material, visible world overtake them, choking out their faith. They become a garden filled with thorns. God's message is crowded out of their lives.

THE joy of the gardener is the fertile soil, the soft soil. This is where the seed can sink in, where it can send roots deep into the soil, where there are very few thorns to stunt the plant's growth.

MOST of our children are soft soil. Child Evangelism Fellowship has made available the results of a survey about the ages at which people become Christians. They say that one percent respond to the salvation message before four years of age. Eighty-five percent come to Jesus when they are between four and fourteen years old. Ten percent are saved between fifteen and thirty years of age. And only 4 percent come into God's kingdom after they are thirty years old (*Children's Ministry Resource Bible.* Nashville: Thomas Nelson, 1994, page 1140).

IT'S obvious that most children have the ears to hear. The soil has not grown hard. Roots have the opportunity to grow deep. And the worries of our material life have not yet overgrown their hearts.

PAUL said, "I planted the seed, Apollos watered it, but God made it grow" (1 Corinthians 3:6). So we plant, we water, and we even try to remove some of the weeds. But it's God who makes the seed grow. In fact, Jesus said, "No one can come to me unless the Father who sent me draws him" (John 6:44). So before we even try to teach God's message, we need to be praying that God will draw our children to Jesus. There are also some things we can do to help prepare the soil. You'll learn how to do this in the first section of this book. There you will find specific ideas for preparing the soil of your children's hearts and establishing an atmosphere in which your teaching will thrive.

THE rest of the book, which focuses on different attributes of God, begins with God as Creator. Although it is not necessary to follow the order of the book or to use every idea, the arrangement that's presented will allow you to teach about God and his kingdom in a very thorough, specific, and organized way.

IT is my prayer that this book will help you and your children grow closer to God and undertake the lifelong adventure of walking with the Holy One as you continuously seek to know him better. "And I pray that Christ will be more and more at home in your hearts as you trust in him. May your roots go down deep into the soil of God's marvelous love. And may you have the power to understand . . . how wide, how long, how high, and how deep his love really is" (Ephesians 3:17-18, NLT).

Milestones

YOU can follow the important milestones in your children's lives, communicating God's message to them in appropriate and understandable ways no matter what their ages are. Learning about four different stages of child development will help you determine the best ways to teach your children about God during each stage. The suggestions here will also guide you as you plan how and when you and your family can use the 100 activities in this book.

Infants

GOD CARES

TEACH your baby that he can trust you to take care of his needs. When baby is hungry, feed him. When she's cold, put a blanket or sweater on her. When baby's diaper is wet, change him. All of this attention gives baby a sense of hope: "No matter how uncomfortable I may feel at this moment, there is someone here to take care of me." This type of modeling is the first way that you will teach your child about God's care. God is faithful. He always provides what we need. So you are faithful to provide for your child's needs. As you change the diaper or wrap the warm blanket around baby, you can say, "I'm taking care of you. God takes care of you."

GOD IS THE CREATOR

TEACH your baby that God is the Creator. As baby eats a piece of banana, say, "God made the banana." Baby tastes the flavor, and you can take that opportunity to introduce baby to God's creative nature. When your baby splashes in the bath, you can say this: "God made water. Thank you, God." Be alert to the experiences that baby enjoys with her eyes, hands, mouth, nose, and ears. Then talk about God, who created the world we enjoy.

GOD LOVES

TEACH your baby that "God is love" (1 John 4:8). When you are hugging and rocking your baby, say, "I love you. God loves you." Baby may not know the words, but he knows the feeling of being loved. You are introducing your baby to God's loving nature.

Early Childhood: Two through Five Years

GOD IS MY FRIEND AND HELPER

YOUNG children often have fears. While some fears are based on reality, other fears are unfounded. However, even unfounded fears feel just as real to the preschooler. Be careful about what you allow your young children to see and hear. Teach them that God understands their fears and has the power to keep them safe. Sing songs about God's love and care. Also read Bible stories that show God's care. Remember that your tender love and care are the real-life translations of God's love and care to your child.

GOD GIVES US RULES TO LIVE BY

YOUNG children are in the process of learning that their actions and words have consequences. Although this is the prime stage for learning what's right and what's wrong, children are not consistent in their ability to correctly choose between right and wrong until they are five or six years old. Tell your preschool children about what God does and does not approve.

Let them know that God gives us rules to live by because he made us and knows what will keep us safe, healthy, and happy. "I will never forget your commandments, for you have used them to restore my joy and health" (Psalm 119:93, NLT).

I CAN READ ABOUT GOD, TALK TO HIM, SING TO HIM

LET your young children see you reading your Bible. Let them hear you pray. Talk naturally about God as your friend and Father. Talk to God spontaneously during the day. Model any other signs of faith that you want them to emulate. They will copy you.

GOD IS REAL

UNTIL children are about five years old, they don't separate fantasy from reality. Tell them when a story is *not* real ("Cinderella," "Spiderman," and so on) and when a story really did happen (Noah and the ark, Jesus heals a blind man, and so on). This will help your children begin thinking about what's real and what's not.

Six through Ten Years

GOD IS ALL-POWERFUL, ALL-WISE, EVER-PRESENT

YOUR children are now dealing personally with more of the world around them. Teach your children that they can rely on God to protect and guide them anywhere and everywhere. Tell your children about what God is doing in your life. Pray with your children about the places they go and the people they know. Continue to help each child see that God is real and active today in the world at large, as well as in the specific events of your child's daily life.

JESUS WANTS TO BE MY SAVIOR

YOUR child's conscience began energizing his decisions in a major way after he turned four years old. Around age five, he began differentiating between fantasy and reality. Now your child is able to think of Bible events in a historical context and understand the order in which biblical events occurred. Your child is also beginning to understand symbolism. And your child is probably more acutely aware that he sins and needs a Savior. Teach your child that all people feel this need. Some people try to fill this need by turning to other things. But only Jesus can satisfy us. Only he can make us sinless and fill us with joy and peace.

Eleven through the Teen Years

GOD IS FAITHFUL

THE teen years are full of questions as young people personalize their faith. They want to be sincere. They don't want to believe simply because it's what Mom and Dad believe or what a youth pastor believes or what a friend believes. They want their faith to be truly their own. They are establishing their own identity and want to be independent in their dependence on God. The teen years also usually bring relationship difficulties that teens need to work through. They are confronted with the reality that all of the people they depend on will let them down sooner or later. No human being is completely faithful. Teach your teens that only God is completely faithful. They can find fulfillment only by depending on God and following his ways.

preparing
the soil

SOMEONE once said, "I'd rather be a fifty-cent rose in seven-dollar soil than a seven-dollar rose in fifty-cent soil." Your relationship with each of your children and the atmosphere you establish in your home or classroom are extremely important. This relationship and atmosphere are the means by which you plow and prepare the soil of your children's hearts so they will be ready to receive God's message.

children are important

1. Communicating Love

Listen to your children: Wait to speak; focus on what they're saying.

Observe your children: Watch them; consider what their actions and reactions tell you about their feelings and beliefs.

Verify what they say: Ask them to explain or tell you more; summarize what they've said to see if you understand.

Enjoy your children: Respect each child as a unique gift from God; value each child's place in your family; value and respect each child's thoughts and feelings. God your Father delights in you. You can model this Father-child relationship as you relate to each of your children.

2. Providing Care

Commitment: Purpose to build a strong relationship with your children.

Availability: Be available to your children; spend time with them.

Rules and responsibilities: Set limits, give reasonable responsibilities, be consistent, and set an example in accepting rules and responsibilities yourself.

Encouragement: Speak words that encourage; give your children hope; allow them to fail and try again.

3. Sharing Time Together

Play Time: Play together in order to strengthen your relationship with each child and to provide a format for communicating and training.

Lunch, Dinner, and Breakfast Time: Eat meals with your children as often as possible. Share ideas and experiences, and encourage each other at the table.

Owl Time: After turning off the lights in each child's room at night, let your child talk to you.

Work Time: Work together in order to strengthen your relationship, to communicate, and to train.

God is important

4. Seeking God Yourself

IMMERSE yourself in God. Seek him. Seek an intimate relationship with him. Immerse yourself in the Bible and mine it, looking carefully for its treasures. Never stop seeking to know God better. Exhibit a hunger and thirst for him. "Love the Lord your God with all your heart and with all your soul and with all your mind" (Matthew 22:37). Whatever your relationship is with God, that's what you will share with your children. "For out of the overflow of the heart the mouth speaks" (Matthew 12:34).

5. Asking Questions

DON'T be afraid to wonder about God. Encourage all of your children to ask questions about God. Don't be afraid to say, "I don't know the answer. I wonder too." Admit that you don't fully understand. Anything that we know and understand is potentially controllable. If we knew and understood all about God, he wouldn't be God. Solomon said, "It is the glory of God to conceal a matter; to search out a matter is the glory of kings" (Proverbs 25:2).

6. Relating Entertainment to God

BE choosy about what you watch and what you allow your children to watch. Debrief informally after watching a show by connecting the theme of the show, or something the characters said and did, with God. Discuss how the values expressed reflect or disagree with his nature and his ways. Try to identify a Bible story with a similar or opposing theme. Listen to what your children have to say about the show. The more informal and brief you can be with your comments, the better, unless the show warrants an in-depth discussion and your children are open to discussing it.

Scripture is important

7. Post-a-Scripture

WRITE simple, meaningful Scriptures on index cards or self-stick notes. Post these in different places around your house: beside a mirror, on a door, on a doorframe, or on a window frame. If some of your children can't read yet, draw a simple picture beside each Scripture. Put one or two Scripture verses up at a time. Change them randomly and periodically, leaving them up long enough for your children to get to know them and to notice when you've changed them.

8. Secret Scriptures

ON an index card, "sticky note," or small piece of paper, write a Scripture verse that you have chosen for your child. Place it under your child's pillow or under the bedspread but on top of the pillow. If your child can't read yet, you can also draw a smiley face or sun or other simple drawing to go with the Scripture. Or put an appropriate sticker on the Scripture card. When your child gets in bed at night, her very own "secret Scripture" is waiting for her. You can do this every night, or just do it one special night a week. Choose Scriptures that are simple, meaningful, and understandable for your child.

9. Family Devotions

BEGIN family devotions with your children even when they are infants, if possible. Tailor your devotional times to fit your needs. Some families find breakfast to be the best time. Others have devotions after dinner. Others have it right before bedtime. Try to set a schedule and be as consistent as possible.

THERE are three kinds of devotions.

- *Story-guided devotions:* You choose a Bible story or Scripture passage to read. Then you discuss and apply the theme of that passage to your lives as individuals or as a family.

- *Topic- or theme-guided devotions:* You choose a topic, such as "honesty," and find a Bible story that fits that theme. You discuss the theme; then read the story to see how the story characters dealt with that theme. Try to link the characters' choices to the consequences they experienced.

- *Activity-guided devotions*: This is especially appropriate for young children. Choose an activity to do as a family. Find a Bible story that complements that activity. For your devotional, do the activity, tell or read the story, and discuss it. For example, build a city with blocks. Tell the story of Jericho, using toy figures if you want. Then talk about how God took care of Rahab. Or bake cookies shaped like stars. Then read or tell the story of the magi (wise men). Talk about how God led the wise men to Jesus. And talk about ways God has led your family.

10. Campfire Time

BUILD a pretend campfire anytime by setting several flashlights in the middle of the floor. Ask your children to build a "campfire" by stacking building blocks as if they were stacking wood. Have them place the blocks on top of the flashlights. (Instead of blocks, you can use cardboard tubes from rolls of gift wrap or paper towels.) Turn the flashlights on, and turn the room lights off. Sit around the "campfire" as you have your family devotional time or as you simply talk and wonder about God.

teaching about God and his kingdom

THE following activities are divided into sections, each of which focuses on one of God's attributes. If you choose activities from each section, you'll find yourself teaching your child about God and his kingdom in a very thorough, specific, and organized way.

God is the Creator

ONE of the mysteries of God is that he has always existed. He is the original artist, scientist, mathematician, and architect. He planned and created all things, even our concept of time. God knows all about everything.

11. Star-Watching

BECOME star-watchers. There's almost nothing that makes us feel our smallness and God's greatness as much as watching the stars. It's a perfect time to wonder about God and to feel his awesome majesty. "The heavens tell of the glory of God. The skies display his marvelous craftsmanship" (Psalm 19:1, NLT). "He determines the number of the stars and calls them each by name" (Psalm 147:4).

12. Stars on the Ceiling

PUT glow-in-the-dark self-stick stars on the ceiling of your child's room. Or place them in another room where you can lie on your backs and gaze up at the overhead picture of the night sky. Talk about God and wonder about him.

13. Travel

IF it's possible, travel with your children to places where you can see some of the wonders of nature: rock formations, seashores, canyons, waterfalls, deserts, forests, caves. Take time to sit and absorb the grandeur and beauty. Thank God for his creation.

14. Animal Watching

OBSERVING animals was the first form of entertainment, and it still has the power to delight and fascinate us. Marvel with your children about the wisdom, creativity, and sense of humor that God displays through the animals he made.

15. Growing a Garden

WE were created to live in a garden. Take time to dig in the dirt, to smell the flowers, and to feel the breeze. Share the awe of watching a butterfly or examining an autumn leaf. Thank the Creator.

16. Walks

TAKE walks with your children, even if you live in the city. Talk about what you see and hear. Talk about God's hand in all of life.

17. Watercolors

PAINT pictures together. Or let your children paint while you read aloud to them. Display their finished pictures. Then ask, "What if someone came to our house and saw the pictures you painted? And what if the person said, 'You didn't do that,' refusing to believe you made the picture? And what if this person said, 'It just happened by accident'? What would you think? How would you feel? How must God feel when people refuse to believe that he created the world?"

God is Father, Son, and Holy Spirit

ANOTHER of God's great mysteries is that he is three in one. "Let us make people in our image," said God in the beginning (Genesis 1:26, NLT). "In the beginning the Word already existed. He was with God, and he was God. . . . So the Word became human and lived here on earth among us. He was full of unfailing love and faithfulness. And we have seen his glory, the glory of the only Son of the Father" (John 1:1, 14, NLT). "Now the Lord is the Spirit" (2 Corinthians 3:17). So when we say "God," we are talking about Father, Son, and Holy Spirit. The following examples are simplistic and inadequate, but they will start thoughts and discussions about the nature of the God who is one, yet three.

18. The Apple

SLICE an apple while your children watch. Take off part of the peeling and show it to your children. Ask them if this is a lemon. Is it a pear? Take a seed out of the apple. Show it to your children. Ask them if these seeds are grapefruit seeds. Are they tomato seeds? What kind of fruit will grow from them? Apples—always. Give your children some of the flesh of the apple to eat. Ask them if it's banana. Is it watermelon? Point to the separate parts of the apple. How can the peeling be apple, the seeds be apple, and the flesh be apple? They are three different parts of the same thing. That's the way it is with the Father, Son, and Holy Spirit. They are each different, but they are all God.

19. Water

LET your children watch as steam comes from water boiling in a pan on the stove. What is steam? It's a form of water. Show your children some ice cubes. What is ice? It's a form of water. How can steam, ice, and water be different but still be the same? They are three different forms of the same thing. That's the way it is with the Father, Son, and Holy Spirit. They are each different, but they are all God.

20. A Letter

WRITE on a piece of paper, "I love you." Sign the letter and place a "seal" by your signature. The seal could be a gold sticker embossed with your initials or a bit of wax dripped on the paper with the impression of a ring or other special object. Or you could even get it notarized. (If you are unable to do any of the above, you can simply print each letter of your first name, printing the second letter on top of the first, the third letter on top of the second, and so on, to form a personal design.) Fold the letter and place it in an envelope. Address it to your children and send it through the mail. When your children get the letter, use it to give this object lesson.

THERE are three parts to this letter:

1. The person who sends it. He thinks and plans what to say.

2. The letter itself—the words that actually tell you the sender's thoughts.

3. The signature and, in this case, the seal proving who the sender is.

THESE three parts represent the three parts of God:

1. God the Father thinks and plans what he wants us to know and be and do.

2. God the Son is the Word (John 1:1, 14). When Jesus came to the earth, he communicated the Father's plans and thoughts.

3. God's Holy Spirit seals the message and proves that God is the one who sent it (Ephesians 1:13-14). He causes an understanding of the message to grow within us (John 14:26).

THERE is a fourth part to the letter: the person who receives it. This person has a choice to believe the words or not believe them. The fourth part represents all the people of the world. God's main message to us is this: "I love you forever." We can choose to believe him or not. Who paid with his life to make it possible for us to receive this message? Just as the stamp is payment for a letter to be sent, Jesus' death was the payment for us to be able to receive God's love for eternity.

21. A Father Has Children

ASK each member of the family to flatten a lump of play dough to make a circle as large as a hand.

(You can use store-bought Play-Doh or make your own by mixing one part salt, one part water, and three parts flour. Add food coloring to make colored dough.) Each family member should then press one of his hands onto the dough circle he made. Talk about how you are all part of the same family even though you are each a different part, and, as your handprints show, you are each unique. God the Father, the Son, and the Holy Spirit were three parts of God in community (family-type) relationship even before he created the world. Read Genesis 1:1-2 and John 1:1-4. Each part is also unique. Yet the three parts form our one God.

READ John 1:12. Believers are children of God. So God is our Father in heaven. Fathers on earth are only human, and sometimes earthly fathers don't treat their children lovingly. Ask your children what their idea of a perfect father would be. How would he treat them? God is a perfect Father who never does wrong, who never stops loving and caring for us.

22. A Father Makes Rules

IF you have a crawling baby or toddler or can arrange to watch a baby for a few hours, ask your children to help you supervise the little one. Take some pictures of your children with the baby. Later, look at the pictures and talk about caring for babies and toddlers. Ask your children what rules they would make for the little one to obey. Why? Ask if they are making those rules just to keep the baby from having fun. Are they making those rules just to be bossy and mean? The rules are to keep the baby safe and healthy. Ask your children to imagine that the baby is quite happy toddling along. But you can see that if baby keeps going, she will soon be in the middle of a busy street. What will you do? Baby might not understand, but you do. So you make a rule (stay away from the street), and you make sure you keep baby away from the street.

GOD, being the good Father that he is, gives us rules to keep us safe and healthy. We might not understand why he makes some of those rules. But we know God sees things we don't see, and he has good reasons for his rules. Ask your children to list some of God's rules and tell why he might have given us those rules.

23. Jesus: God with Us

ASK each of your children to think of a real person, historical or living now, whom your child has never met but would like to meet someday. (Young children may choose fictional characters since they sometimes have difficulty knowing whether a character is real or not. That's OK.) No one can tell anyone who the person is. Have one child let the others guess the name of the chosen person. Each person asks this child a question about the identity of the person, but the question can have only a yes or no answer. For example, "Is this person a man?" If no one guesses the identity of the secret person within ten guesses, the child tells who his secret person is. After the game, talk about the possibility of meeting the people everyone chose. Do you know your chosen person very well right now?

Would you know that person better if you actually spent some time with him or her? Jesus came to earth to spend time with us and to let us know what God is like. In fact, the Bible calls Jesus "Immanuel," which means "God with us" (Matthew 1:23). What was Jesus like? He did only what he knew his Father wanted. He showed us that God is love.

24. God's Holy Spirit: Unseen Power

GET a Ping-Pong ball and a hair blow-dryer. Turn the blow-dryer to a low setting and aim the stream of air upward. Place the ball in the stream of air close to the nozzle of the dryer. The ball will sit suspended in the stream of air. With the ball still in the air stream, turn the dryer to medium and then to high. The ball floats in the air. Ask your children if they can see the air. They can't see it, but it is real and powerful.

SET a battery-operated radio on the table and gather around it. Tell your children about radio waves that travel through the air. Can we see them? No, but they are all around us. They are real and powerful. Turn on the radio to pick up the waves and amplify them. You can do the same with the television as it picks up pictures that come from a distance as far away as the satellites.

NOW talk about the Holy Spirit. *Holy* means "different and godly." *Spirit* means "invisible being." The Holy Spirit is beyond what we can see. But he is real, and he is the power who works out God's will around us and in us.

IF you want to read some Bible verses or some stories from *God's Story* about how the Holy Spirit empowered people, try these:

- *Samson* (Judges 14–15, "Honey from a Lion" and "Fighting with a Jaw Bone," pages 116 and 118 in *God's Story*)

- *Saul* (1 Samuel 10, "Long Live Our King!" page 131 in *God's Story*)

- *David* (1 Samuel 16, "Choosing the Next King," page 137 in *God's Story*)

- *Mary* (Luke 1:35, "A Message for Mary," page 504 in *God's Story*)

- *Jesus* (Luke 4:14, "Jesus' Home Town," page 520 in *God's Story*)

- *Peter and the other believers* (Acts 2, "Wind, Fire, and Different Languages," page 633 in *God's Story*)

- *All believers* (Ephesians 3:16, "Wide, Long, High, and Deep," page 740 in *God's Story*)

25. God's Holy Spirit: Our Power Source

GIVE your children a flashlight that has no batteries inside, but don't tell them it has no batteries. Darken the room and ask them to turn the flashlight on. When it won't come on, turn the room lights back on and let the children discover that the flashlight has no batteries. Put some marbles in the flashlight. Act as if you are confident that this will solve the problem. Turn the room lights off and try the flashlight again. Keep trying other objects instead of batteries for awhile. Finally place batteries in the flashlight.

TELL your children that God created each of us to be a home for his Holy Spirit. Believers are temples of the Holy Spirit (1 Corinthians 6:19). For us to be all God meant us to be, we have to be filled with God the Holy Spirit, just like the flashlight had to be filled with batteries to work. The Holy Spirit works to grow the wisdom of God in us. Jesus called him the "Counselor" (John 14:26). The Holy Spirit of God also works to grow the character and purity of God in us (Galatians 5:22-23).

26. The Holy Spirit: God's Seal of Ownership

GIVE your children some play dough or clay and some small objects to press into the clay to make a design. Tell your children about the way kings used to put their seals on special messages they sent. The king's seal was often made of wax. The wax was placed on the message. Then the king pressed a special ring called a "signet ring" into the wax. The Pharaoh gave Joseph his signet ring when he chose Joseph to be in charge of

Egypt. Even today, we have special documents "sealed" or marked. Show your children a birth certificate or marriage certificate or other notarized document. Explain that a notary seal is a proof that this document is authentic. In the same way, the Holy Spirit in you is proof that God is real and you are truly his child (Ephesians 1:13).

God is holy and awesome

MANY aspects of God are a mystery to us: his invisibility, his power, his majesty, and his glory. In short, God is awesome and unique. In a sense, the word *holy* means "unique." It means "set apart" and "different." It also means "perfect, pure, and sinless." There is no one like God. He alone is worthy of our praise and worship. (See Revelation 15:4.)

27. How Does God Describe Himself?

ASK your children to describe themselves as if they were introducing themselves to a new friend and telling something about themselves. Describe yourself to your children in the same way. Say, "I wonder how God describes himself." Then read Exodus 33:18–34:8, "Moses Sees God's Back" and "Two More Stone Charts," pages 71 and 72 in *God's Story*. This is what God wanted Moses to know about him. This is God describing himself. Ask your children if God has changed since that time. Here is the answer: "I am the Lord, and I do not change" (Malachi 3:6, NLT).

28. Discovering God

GO on a "discovery tour" through Psalms during family devotional times.

Give each child a blank spiral notebook. Take one psalm a day. You may want to take several days to cover some of the longer psalms. Ask your children to listen carefully as you read each psalm. Ask them to write down any name of God that they hear and any description of God that they hear. After you have finished the reading, compare lists and discuss what your children learned about God.

29. Eyewitness Accounts

ASK all of the people in your family to describe the most famous person they have ever seen. Or read a newspaper or magazine article in which a reporter describes a famous person. Very few people have seen God, and even then they didn't see God in all his fullness. But what they did see was awesome. Read Isaiah 6:1-5 and Revelation 4. If these descriptions sound scary, review how God describes himself in Exodus 33:18—34:7a.

30. The Wind

WAVE a piece of stiff cardboard like a fan in the air so that it blows "wind" on your child. If you have a pinwheel, blow it to make it spin. Look outside and see if the wind is blowing leaves or flags or clouds. Ask your child if she can see the wind. The wind is invisible. We can't see the wind. But we can see what it does. We can feel it too. God is also invisible. But he is very real. We can see what God does. And we can feel him loving us. Read Psalm 46:10: "Be still, and know that I am God." Then sit still and think about God. Feel him loving you.

31. False Gods

IF you have travel magazines, geographic magazines, or an encyclopedia, find pictures of idols. Many people who are not Christians believe in a god. If we tell them we believe in God, they say, "I believe in God, too." But they are not thinking of the one true God. Ask your children what makes our God different from these other gods. Read Deuteronomy 3:23-24; 4:1-8; Isaiah 64:4.

THERE are other kinds of false gods or idols that you may want to discuss with your older children. Talk about what worship is.

Read Romans 12:1-2. Notice that Paul says giving ourselves to God is our spiritual worship. If we accept that as a broad definition of worship, what are some other things that people, even Christians, give their lives to? Is it possible to "worship" money? Discuss what God can do for you that other things we worship can't do.

32. A to Z Descriptions

GET a roll of butcher paper, shelf paper, or calculator tape. Or tape several pieces of plain white paper together end to end to make a long strip. Hang this long paper vertically on a wall. Ask your children to write the letters of the alphabet in a column down the left side of the paper. Then go down the alphabet column together, writing one word that starts with each letter and describes God. For example: Awesome, Brilliant, Caring, and so on. When you get to X, you may use a word that starts with ex.

33. Our Own Psalms

ONLY God is worthy of our praise and worship. Read some praise and worship psalms. These are some you may want to consider:

- *Psalm 33:1–11* ("A New Song," page 202 in *God's Story*)
- *Psalm 84* ("Even the Sparrow," page 196 in *God's Story*)
- *Psalm 95:1–7* ("The Deep Earth in His Hand," page 189 in *God's Story*)
- *Psalm 104* ("Earth, Sea, and Moon," page 206 in *God's Story*).

THEN, as a family, write your own psalm of praise, telling God in your own words how great he is.

God is always near

GOD is available. He is with us everywhere we go. He listens at any time, in any place.

34. Spontaneous Prayers

LET children "catch" you talking to your Father. As you go through your day, speak short prayers. "Father, thank you for those beautiful clouds." "Guide me through this traffic, Lord." "Praise you, Father. You helped Shawna through her recital."

35. Planned Prayer Time

ESTABLISH a private prayer time for yourself. If your children are old enough to supervise themselves at this time, you may want to close the door to your room. Pray out loud. Tell your children they may interrupt by walking in quietly or gently tapping on your door if they need you. They will know that you are talking to your Father. Your example will be a stronger teacher than your words.

36. Unlimited Prayers

PRAY about anything and everything. Go to God in times of stress, anger, grief, disappointment, worry, joy, anticipation, gratitude, and accomplishment. This shows your children that you are confident that God cares, hears, and answers.

God rules the kingdom of light

GOD'S kingdom is called the "kingdom of light" (Colossians 1:12). "God is light; in him there is no darkness at all" (1 John 1:5). He wants us to choose to join this kingdom to receive his joy, peace, and love—now and for eternity.

37. Light Shines in the Darkness

TURN off the lights and read John 1:1-14 by the light of a candle or a flashlight. Reread verse 5. Talk about the powerful nature of light. Explain that light can get rid of darkness, but darkness cannot get rid of light. Once the light is on, darkness cannot overcome it. Darkness is gone, for it is the absence of light, not a power, that overtakes light. It's the same way in the spiritual world. The kingdom of darkness can rule only where the kingdom of light has not been allowed to come. When we ask Jesus to be our Lord, we have asked the true Light to rule in our lives. His presence takes away the darkness.

38. Shaping Images with Clay or Play-Doh

AS you manipulate the clay, talk about the fact that God created us in his image. Discuss what that means. Then talk about what happened after Adam and Eve sinned. Sin separated them from God. Then people who did not follow God found themselves in a spiritual kingdom of darkness, where they were being shaped by the world. It's still that way today. Before we believe in Jesus as our Savior, worldly forces are shaping our lives.

39. Mud and Water

FILL a small jar with very muddy water. Fill another small jar with clear water. Show both jars to your children and ask which they would rather swim in. Being in the world is like swimming in muddy water. We get the "dirt" of sin on us. But if we know Jesus, we can be pure and clean in the world. That's because we are living in his spiritual kingdom, and he has forgiven our sins. (See 1 John 1:9; 2:15; 4:1, 4.)

40. The Umbrella

OPEN an umbrella and hold it. Tell your children that the umbrella represents God's protection, which he gives to those who are in his kingdom, the kingdom of light.

If you are not in the light, what are you in? Darkness. Those who have chosen not to place themselves under God's authority find themselves automatically in the kingdom of darkness, where Satan is in charge. There is no other choice. Those who have not chosen God are living in Satan's realm. Satan lies, steals, kills, and destroys (John 8:44; 10:10). There is no protection from evil unless we choose to come into God's kingdom by receiving Jesus as our Lord and Savior. (Step under the umbrella.) Then God is our shield, our deliverer, and our protector (Psalm 18:2).

God saves us

MANY people have the idea that God is a condemning God—that he's angry and scowling, keeping score of our good and bad deeds, ready to judge us. God does want us to live pure lives. But the Bible tells us that "God did not send his Son into the world to condemn the world, but to save the world through him. Whoever believes in him is not condemned, but whoever does not believe stands condemned already" (John 3:17-18). By default, we find ourselves in the kingdom of darkness if we don't choose to live in God's kingdom. God loved us so much, he couldn't bear to leave us in darkness where we were condemned. So he sent his Son to save us by taking the blame and punishment for our sins.

41. The Magnet and the Paper Clip

SET a strong magnet down on a table. Tie a ten-inch piece of string to a paper clip. Set the paper clip on the table out of reach of the magnet's pull. Lay the string out on the table so that it's pointing away from the magnet. Now tape the end of the string to the table and slowly move the magnet toward the paper clip. When the magnetic force pulls the paper clip toward the magnet, stop moving the magnet so that the paper clip is being drawn to the magnet, but is not yet touching it.

THE magnet represents God's love. We are the paper clip. The string is sin. God's love draws us to him, but sin keeps us separated. Sin "entangles" us

(Hebrews 12:1) and holds us back. That's why God sent Jesus. Jesus came to take the blame for our sins. He took our punishment at the cross. (Untie the string from the paper clip, allowing the clip to be pulled to the magnet.) When we trust Jesus as our Savior, he frees us from our sins and puts us in right relationship with God again.

42. Layers of Clothes

SIN in our lives can become like layers of baggage that weigh us down. Let your children list some common sins (lying, greed, pride, fear, and so on). Write each sin on a slip of paper. Now pin the slips of paper to the outside back of different items of clothing that a child can put on over his arms (vests, shirts, windbreaker jackets, heavier jacket, coat). Talk about how one sin leads to another. Place the vest on a child. Read the name of the sin that is pinned to it. Continue placing the other items on the same child, layering them one on top of the other. It helps if the heavier items of clothing are larger in size and if you layer the clothes by starting with the lightest item and ending with the heaviest. Sin weighs us down. It's hard to do anything productive when we are weighed down with sin. How do we get rid of sin in our lives? As you discuss forgiveness, God's love in sending his Son, Jesus' death, and his resurrection, remove the layers one at a time. "Let us strip off every weight that slows us down, especially the sin that so easily hinders our progress" (Hebrews 12:1, NLT).

43. The Jail

MAKE a "jail" by using six pieces of black ribbon, each about three feet long, and two sticks or dowels, each also about three feet long. Using black electrical or fabric tape, tape one end of each ribbon to one stick, spacing the ribbons evenly. Then tape the other end of each ribbon to the other stick. Hold the "jail" up in front of you or a child and talk about the trap of sin. Talk about how we can't get out by ourselves, but Jesus sets us free. He took the punishment for our sins.

44. The Mousetrap

SHOW children a mousetrap or a rat trap. Place a piece of cheese on it. (You may not want to set the trap because it's quite painful if it's accidentally tripped and snaps a finger. Supervise carefully and be very cautious.) Talk about how good a piece of cheese looks to a mouse. The mouse is tempted. If he gives in to temptation, he is trapped. Relate this to the way we see temptation. What are some things that tempt us? These things look good to us. If we give in to temptation, we are trapped by sin. Who can save us? The lesson is the same as in "The Jail."

45. Chains and Handcuffs

SHOW children some chains and/or handcuffs. A child may want to volunteer to be handcuffed. (Keep the keys handy!) The Bible says we are slaves to sin (John 8:34; Romans 6:16; 2 Peter 2:19). What does it mean to be a slave? What does it mean to be a slave to sin? Who sets us free? How? Have you ever heard anyone say that we are bought with Jesus' blood? That means we once belonged to the world and were slaves to sin, but Jesus' death set us free.

46. Coupons

SHOW your child some grocery coupons. Take the coupons to the store and use them to buy something. This is called "redeeming" your coupons. You are a "redeemer" because you are redeeming your coupons. That is, you are trading in the coupons to buy something. The Bible says that Jesus is our Redeemer. He traded his life to buy us so that we could be God's children. His death was the payment to redeem us from being slaves to sin.

47. Saving an Animal

IF you want a pet, save one from an animal shelter. You are now the savior of that animal. Compare this experience to the way God sent Jesus to us to save us from sin and death. Point out that Jesus is the only Savior who can give us eternal life.

48. The Slate

GET two "magic slates," commonly used by children to write on with the plastic or wooden stick provided. Lifting up the plastic overlay automatically erases the drawing. Show your children one of the slates with no marks on it. Talk about how our sins are like marks against us. Let your children list some sins. Every time a sin is named, the child naming the sin must make a mark on the slate. Then talk about the impossibility of being able to save ourselves. On our own, we could never become perfect. We could never have a right relationship with God. So God sent Jesus. Show the second slate, which has no marks. Jesus was perfect. But he took our sins. Jesus came to take the blame for us. Let each child make a mark on the unmarked slate. Then lift the plastic overlay on the first slate. This represents us. Now, as God sees it, it's just as if we'd never sinned. Jesus traded his purity for our sinfulness. He died as the punishment for our sins. Then he came back to life, overpowering sin. Lift the overlay on the second slate. Now God the Son lives in heaven with God the Father and is no longer covered with our sins.

49. The Paper Cup

PLACE a paper cup on the palm of your outstretched hand. Tell your children that the cup represents Adam. Your palm represents God. In the beginning, Adam had a very close relationship with God. God walked and talked with Adam. God took care of Adam and gave Adam everything he needed. But then Adam disobeyed God. He chose not to trust God. Adam sinned. Sin separates us from God. (Place the cup on the floor. Keep your hand extended, palm up.)

HOW can the cup get back up into the hand? Look at the cup and tell it to jump up into your hand. Tell it two or three times to jump into your hand. It can't. All people are separated from God by sin. People try to get back into a relationship with God in many ways. But people can't do it. That's why God sent Jesus. (Reach down and pick up the cup, placing it back on your palm.) Through Jesus, God came to earth to bring us back into friendship with him. Now we can walk and talk with God, and God takes care of us. He gives us everything we need. And someday we will live even closer to God—in heaven! Jesus became the way for us to come back to God.

50. Our Sins Are Nailed to the Cross

MAKE a small wooden cross by nailing or tying together two pieces of wood, two feet by four feet. Give each person a small piece of paper. Ask everyone to write one of his sins on the piece of paper. No one has to show the paper to anyone else. The paper should be folded so no one can see the writing. Then each person has a turn nailing his piece of paper to the cross as you read this verse: "He personally carried away our sins in his own body on the cross so we can be dead to sin and live for what is right. You have been healed by his wounds!" (1 Peter 2:24, NLT).

51. Stories

- **TELL** your children the story of how you came to believe in Jesus.

- **THINK** of people you know who have strong testimonies of how they came to salvation. Ask them to come over for dinner. As you talk around the dinner table, ask them to share their testimonies.

- **ASK** missionaries who are home on furlough to visit your family for a meal. Have them tell some of their experiences of sharing the salvation message in other lands.

- **ENCOURAGE** grandmothers and grandfathers to share their testimonies.

52. The Message in Your Hand

TELL the following action story.

HOLD up your thumb. Ask, "Who is the greatest of all?" God is. God is perfect.

HOLD up your pointer finger. Point to yourself, then to your child. "Am I perfect? Are you? No. We are not."

HOLD up the pointer finger and thumb to make a J shape. "That's why God sent Jesus. Jesus came to take the blame for the wrong things we do."

CROSS your right pointer finger horizontally over your left pointer finger to make a cross. "Jesus died on the cross as punishment for our sins."

HOLD both hands out, palms up. "Now we can be perfect. This is God's gift to us."

FOLD hands as if to pray. "If we want this gift, all we have to do is ask."

53. Remembering

GET a shoebox or a basket. Into the box or basket, place small items that would cause your children to remember an experience: a birthday candle, an empty medicine bottle, a Christmas ornament, a Valentine card, and so on. Ask each child to choose one item and tell what occasion the item helps her remember. Then talk about communion: the bread and wine. Jesus gave these to us to help us remember what he did for us. Read 1 Corinthians 11:23-26.

54. What the Bible Says

READ and discuss the following passages from *God's Story* to show your children the salvation message in simple, understandable terms.

"Coming Back to Life" page 689 (1 Corinthians 15)

"Even If Every Person Lies" page 704 (Romans 3)

"At the Right Time" page 706 (Romans 5)

"More than Winners" page 708 (Romans 8)

"Kingdom of Light" page 733 (Colossians 1)

"Born to Do Good Things" page 739 (Ephesians 2)

"Richer than Gold" page 769 (1 Peter 1)

"Jesus' Brothers and Sisters" page 780 (Hebrews 2)

"Better Gifts" page 784 (Hebrews 9)

God is merciful and forgiving

GOD would not be perfect and just if he let people get away with sin. But God is also merciful and loving. He made us and does not want anyone to remain separated from him because of sin. So God achieved perfect justice and mercy at the cross. Justice was served because there was punishment for our sin. But mercy was given because it was Jesus who was punished for us, taking our place. We are now forgiven. We can receive that forgiveness by believing in Jesus, or we can refuse that forgiveness by refusing to believe in Jesus.

55. Confessing and Repenting

APOLOGIZE to your children when you have done something wrong, and let your children hear you confessing your sin to God in prayer. This gives them an example for confessing their own sins and repenting before you and the Lord. It also shows your children that you have the faith to believe God forgives you. Let your children know that "if we confess our sins, he is faithful and just and will forgive us our sins and purify us from all unrighteousness" (1 John 1:9). When your children apologize to you, be gracious in the same way that God is by telling them you forgive them.

56. Granting Mercy

OCCASIONALLY, when your child has done something he knows is wrong and when your child knows he deserves to be punished for the wrong that was done, give your child mercy. Say, "Here's what you did that was wrong. You deserve to be punished now. But I'm giving you mercy instead because Jesus gave me mercy."

57. Bleached Heart

SPREAD a sheet of red tissue paper over a white plastic disposable plate or a disposable aluminum pie tin. Pour a small amount of bleach into a small bowl. Give your children cotton swabs. Tell them to dip the cotton swabs into the bleach and gently paint the bleach on the tissue paper in the shape of hearts. Read Isaiah 1:18: "Though your sins are like scarlet, they shall be as white as snow; though they are red as crimson, they shall be like wool."

58. East and West

USING a globe, ask your children to point out where you live. Ask them to show you where east is. Ask them to show you where west is. Using the globe, show your children how you can go east, but east is still east of you. Or you can go west, but west is still west of you. East and west never meet. Read Psalm 103 aloud to your children. Ask what this psalm tells them about God.

Then reread verses 11 and 12. God has separated our sins from us as far as the east is from the west. That means we are sinless.

59. Pepper and Water

FILL a bowl with clean water. Sprinkle a bit of pepper on top. Tell your children that the pepper represents sin. Let them name some sins that children might have. Let each child sprinkle a little more pepper on the water. Who can take away our sins? Jesus can. He took the blame and the punishment for our sins. Place a drop or two of liquid dishwashing detergent in the water. The pepper will immediately rush to the sides of the bowl, leaving the center clear again. Jesus took our sins away. God has forgiven us.

60. A New Canvas

DRAW, color, or paint a picture while your children do the same. Then, using your picture as an example, talk about how God created the world to be a perfect place. But then Adam and Eve sinned. Take a dark color and make a jagged line through your picture. Adam and Eve's world was no longer perfect. They had disobeyed God. We all sin and disobey God. Sin messes up our lives. But God sent Jesus to take away our sins. Now we can have a new start, free from sin. Show a new piece of paper on which you can draw or paint. "If anyone is in Christ, he is a new creation; the old has gone, the new has come!" (2 Corinthians 5:17).

61. The Broken Heart

EVERYONE has two kinds of hearts.

Draw a heart. One kind of heart is the muscle that pumps blood through our bodies. You can feel this heart beat by putting your hand on your chest. The other "heart" we talk about is the part of us that thinks and feels. It feels a dirty, bad feeling when we do wrong.

Draw a horizontal line across the center of the heart. Our heart gets hurt and broken by the bad choices we make and sometimes by the bad choices other people make. Who can mend our broken hearts?

Starting at the bottom and going through the top, draw a vertical line through the center of the heart. *This makes a cross.* God can forgive us because Jesus took the blame and was punished on the cross for our sins. What Satan meant for evil, God can turn into good.

62. Getting a Gift

WRAP a gift box. It can be an empty box, or it can be an actual gift for your child. (If you prefer, use money—five dollars or more.) Stand across the room from your child. Ask your child to suppose that this wrapped box or money is a gift for her. Ask if she has the gift yet. What if she does not come to get it? What if the gift stays on the shelf? Is the gift doing the child any good? Ask your child what she needs to do to have this gift that is being freely given to her. She must receive it, accept it, open it. God freely offers us the gift of eternal life, but we must choose whether to receive it or not. God honors our choice and gives us what we have chosen.

God is perfect and righteous

GOD is perfect and righteous (right in all he does and says). God allows nothing imperfect, wrong, or sinful to live in his presence. God wants us to be perfect and holy so that we can live with him (Leviticus 11:45). But we are imperfect and sinful. So how are we able to live in his presence? How are we able to come before his throne in prayer? The answer, of course, is Jesus.

63. The Passport

IF you have a passport, show it to your children. Talk about how it allows you to enter other countries. Without it, you are not allowed to go into these countries. Compare having a passport to having Jesus as Savior. Jesus gave his life for us so that we can live in God's presence. Receiving Jesus as our Lord and Savior becomes a passport that allows us to live in God's presence. In fact, that's one reason we pray "in Jesus' name, Amen." Jesus' name gives our prayers power and authority before God the Father.

64. The Press Pass

BEFORE a reporter is allowed to cover a sports event or political event, he must be issued a Press Pass. This lets him get into secured, guarded areas where he would otherwise not be allowed to go. The lesson is the same as described in the previous lesson, "The Passport."

65. Torn Jeans

SHOW a pair of old torn jeans or "cutoffs." Ask your children to imagine that they are playing ball in their old jeans and getting them very dirty. Mom calls them to come in and get cleaned up because the family is going to go to Aunt Susan's formal wedding. Will Mom let you go to the wedding in the dirty, torn jeans you are wearing? No. In a comparable way, sin makes our heart dirty. We cannot live in God's presence with a dirty heart. So Jesus "washes" our hearts clean from sin. Only Jesus can make us clean and sinless because no one else is sinless. He is God, so he is perfect and pure and clean.

66. Washing Hands

WHEN your hands or your children's hands are dirty and it's time to wash up, talk about how it's usually easy to clean our hands by washing with soap and water. Ask your children if they've ever felt dirty or bad inside themselves when they've done something wrong. That's guilt. When we sin, we feel dirty in our heart. Is that something we can wash off with soap and water? No. We have to ask God to forgive us. Only Jesus can make us clean from sin.

67. The Car Wash

WHEN your car is dirty, take your children with you to the car wash. Talk about how our lives as sinners are like dirty cars. But when we come to Jesus, he cleans us from our sins. Seeing our clean car coming out of the car wash reminds us of how Jesus cleans us from sin (Psalm 51:7; Isaiah 1:18).

68. No Service

POINT out the signs that say "No shirt, no shoes—no service" on the windows of fast food restaurants. Can you get into that restaurant without a shirt and shoes? No. In fact there are fancy restaurants that won't allow men to come inside unless they are wearing suits and ties. We can't come into God's kingdom unless we are perfect and holy. So how can we live with God? Jesus came to take the blame for our sins. He was punished for our sins when he died on the cross. If we accept his death for us and receive him as our Savior, it's just as if we never sinned. Then we can be in God's kingdom.

69. The Scepter

READ the story of Esther aloud to your children. *God's Story* contains a simple, understandable retelling of the story on pages 476–483. You can read it in one sitting, or read a bit each day for a week. When you've finished the story, call your children's attention back to the time when Esther approached the king without knowing whether he would allow her to come in to see him or not. He held out his scepter, his gold rod, to show that Esther had his permission to approach him. Tell your children that God is our King, and he is better than Queen Esther's king or any other king. God is perfect. He does not allow anyone who sins to live with him. So we cannot come into his presence on our own because we sin. We do wrong. But Jesus came to take the blame for our sins. He was punished for our sins so that we can be sinless. Now we can come into his presence, just as Esther came into the king's presence. God says, "Come on in. I love you. I welcome you. Come and be with me."

70. The Curtain

GET an old piece of cloth—an old sheet or pillowcase will work. Read Exodus 26:31-33; use the piece of cloth as an example of the curtain that separated the Holy Place from the Most Holy Place. Read Hebrews 9:1-7 to learn that no one but the high priest could go into the Most Holy Place. Then read Matthew 27:50-51 to show what happened when Jesus died. Tear the cloth apart from the top to the bottom. Ask your children who tore the curtain that was in front of the Most Holy Place. Why? God tore it to show that we can all come to God now because Jesus was punished for our sins when he died, making us holy and sinless.

God is faithful

GOD will never stop loving us. God is our provider. He is our strength. He has given us all we need (2 Peter 1:3). We can do nothing in our own strength. We must draw from God's abundance (John 15:5). We depend on him. And God is dependable. He is worthy of our trust. He will never let us down.

71. The Candle That Won't Stop Burning

LIGHT a trick candle, the kind that can't be blown out. (Follow the instructions on the package. You may need to light the candle and let it burn a minute before you start this object lesson.) With the candle burning, tell your children that this flame represents God's love. Does he ever stop loving us? What if we do something wrong? (Ask a child to blow the flame out. It will quickly come back again.) He still loves us. What if we do something else wrong? (Blow out the candle.) God still loves us. God will never stop loving us. He is faithful. And that makes us want to do our best to be faithful to him.

72. The Blessings of Being Blameless

OPEN a discussion with your children about blaming others, and direct the discussion toward what it means for someone to take the blame or get the blame. Then talk about Jesus taking the blame for our wrongs. If Jesus took the blame for our sins, then we are blameless. God has some very special promises for those who are blameless. (And that's us!) Read the following Scriptures to your children. If your children are older, they can look up other Scriptures about blame in a concordance. What do these Scriptures tell you about our God?

- The days of the blameless are known to the Lord, and their inheritance will endure forever (Psalm 37:18).

- For the Lord God is a sun and shield; the Lord bestows favor and honor; no good thing does he withhold from those whose walk is blameless (Psalm 84:11).

- For the Lord gives wisdom, and from his mouth come knowledge and understanding. He holds victory in store for the upright, he is a shield to those whose walk is blameless (Proverbs 2:6-7).

- For the upright will live in the land, and the blameless will remain in it (Proverbs 2:21).

- The Lord . . . delights in those whose ways are blameless" (Proverbs 11:20).

- The blameless will receive a good inheritance (Proverbs 28:10).

- He whose walk is blameless is kept safe (Proverbs 28:18).
- He will keep you strong to the end, so that you will be blameless on the day of our Lord Jesus Christ (1 Corinthians 1:8).
- For he chose us in him before the creation of the world to be holy and blameless in his sight (Ephesians 1:4).

73. Ebenezers

GOD'S people often set up a stone memorial to help them remember an occasion when God was faithful to help them. Jacob did this (Genesis 28, "A Ladder up to Heaven," page 25 in *God's Story*). Joshua did this (Joshua 3–5, "The River Stops Flowing," page 96 in *God's Story*). It was Samuel who first called this type of memorial an *Ebenezer*, which means "stone of help" (1 Samuel 7, "Fighting with Thunder," page 128 in *God's Story*).

AT a time when God shows himself faithful to you and your family in a special way, choose an object to be an Ebenezer for your family. It can symbolize God's faithfulness in that situation. Periodically, retell some of the ways God has shown himself faithful to you and your family. Your children can help you remember. Looking at family photo albums sometimes brings back memories of God's faithfulness.

74. Shadows

ON a sunny day when you are outdoors, watch shadows grow shorter or longer as the sun crosses the sky. Let your children place a marker at the spot where they are standing. You mark the spot where their shadows end. Every fifteen or twenty minutes, your children can go back to the same spot where they stood at first, and you can mark the length of their shadows again. Read or tell your children about the verse in the Bible that says that God "does not change like shifting shadows" (James 1:17). Ask your children to tell you some of their favorite unchanging characteristics of God. Read Hebrews 13:8.

75. The Rock

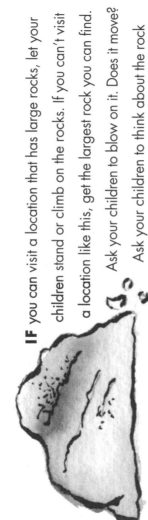

IF you can visit a location that has large rocks, let your children stand or climb on the rocks. If you can't visit a location like this, get the largest rock you can find.

Ask your children to blow on it. Does it move?

Ask your children to think about the rock on which they are blowing or standing. If the wind blows on it, will the wind blow it away? No. The big rock stays right there. It does not move. The Bible sometimes calls God our Rock (Deuteronomy 32:4; 1 Samuel 2:2; Psalm 18:2). That's because God is faithful. No matter what happens, he will never stop loving you. He will never move away from you. He has promised to be with you always. Read Joshua 1:9.

76. A Cup in the Hand

ASK your child to hold her hand out flat, palm up. Set a small paper cup on your child's outstretched palm. Ask your child to blow on it. It will blow off of her hand. The cup is not steady. This is like a person who does not believe in Jesus. That person is "like a wave of the sea, blown and tossed by the wind" (James 1:6). Set the cup on your child's outstretched palm again. This time ask your child to hold on to the cup and blow on it again. Does it fall this time? When we believe in Jesus, he holds on to us. We are "steadfast": steady and fastened down. In fact, Jesus said, "My sheep [that's us!] listen to my voice; I know them, and they follow me. . . . No one can snatch them out of my hand" (John 10:27-28). God is faithful.

77. The Cornerstone

HELP your children use their blocks to build two walls connected at the corner. (If you don't have blocks, you can use paper cups turned upside down. Stack them so that each cup on the upper rows spans two below it.) Point out the block on the bottom row at the corner. That's the "cornerstone." The other blocks depend on that block to hold them up. The Bible tells us that Jesus is the "cornerstone" of God's family (Ephesians 2:20). Jesus loved us so much that he saved us by dying for our sins. So we can depend on Jesus. He's the reason we can be in God's family. Ask one of your children to pull the cornerstone out from the wall you built. What happens? Can anything take Jesus' love and support away from us? Read Romans 8:38-39. Jesus is faithful.

78. Guests

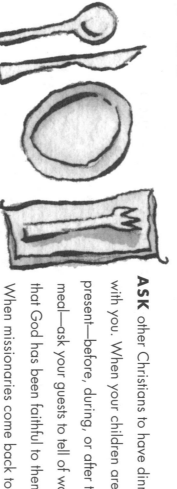

ASK other Christians to have dinner with you. When your children are present—before, during, or after the meal—ask your guests to tell of ways that God has been faithful to them.

When missionaries come back to visit your congregation, ask them to visit your house for dinner. Ask them to tell what God is doing in the country in which they have been living and how God has shown himself faithful to them. In turn, you and your family can tell your dinner guests how God has been faithful to you.

79. Go to God

GO to God in prayer yourself in times of stress, anger, grief, disappointment, worry, joy, or accomplishment. Ask your children to pray for you. By doing this, you show your children that you depend on God and trust him to be faithful no matter what the circumstances of life may be. You are the model for your children.

Act to be copied; speak to be echoed.

80. Wise Sayings

DEVELOP wise sayings or family proverbs to fit the situations in which your family finds itself. These sayings should be encouraging. They should be a testimony of your family's faith in God. For example, in the midst of a move or when your children are anxious about going somewhere, the family proverb might be: "No matter where, God is there." Or: "God's in control wherever we go." In times of financial insecurity you might say: "It's God who clothes and God who feeds, and he'll provide for all our needs." Repeat these proverbs from time to time when appropriate. Your children can write them down and turn them into a family book of proverbs, illustrating each proverb with their own artwork or photographs.

81. Scripture Memory

AS a family, memorize Scriptures that apply to situations you and your children are facing right now. For example, if your child has fears, you might memorize these words together: "In God I trust; I will not be afraid" (Psalm 56:11). Older children can search a concordance for Scriptures that your family can memorize. Have them look for topics related to finances, honesty, the words you speak to each other, and other family needs.

God is our wise teacher

GOD is wise. He has given us the Bible as the foundational book that tells us about himself. Through the Bible, God also teaches us how to live wisely—how to live in ways that please him and bring blessings into our lives.

82. Turning on the Lights

TURN the lights off. If it is still light, pull the shades or drapes to darken the room. Ask your children how often they turn the lights on in the house. Ask them why they turn the lights on.

Psalm 119:105 says, "Your word is a lamp to my feet and a light for my path." When we don't read the Bible, it's as if we are leaving the lights off. What would happen after dark if we left the lights off at home? We would bump into things. We wouldn't be able to see where we're going. It's the same way in our lives. If we don't read the Bible, we bump into hard times that we could have avoided. We can't see where we are headed in life. Can you imagine turning on the lights at home only once a week? You need them every night. But some

people read God's Word only one time a week—and that's usually on Sunday

at church.

83. The Treasure

TREAT your Bible as a precious treasure. For infants and toddlers, pat your Bible gently as you tell them, "Pat the Bible." Holding one of your little one's hands, show how to gently pat the Bible. Hug your Bible, and give the child a small Bible to hug. Continue to treat your Bible as a treasured possession as your children grow up. Let them see you reading your Bible and keeping it available. When God shows you something interesting in your Bible reading, tell your children what God taught you.

84. Standing in the Way

STAND in a darkened room with a flashlight. Ask a child to stand beside you and hold your hand. Walk around the room. Now ask the child to pretend he is not content to go at your pace; he'd rather go faster, or he'd rather choose his own direction. Ask him to step out in front of you. Now he's in front of the flashlight, blocking the light. Can he see the path anymore? No. God asks us to walk with him or to follow him. He knows the way we should go. When we get impatient and run ahead of God, we get confused about the way to go. If we decide to go in a direction that's different from where God is going, we move into the darkness.

85. Children's Bibles

IF your child is too young to read, get him a preschool Bible with pictures that he will like. The text should be easy for him to understand if you read it to him. When your child is learning to read, get her an easy reader Bible storybook. Let her read to you and to younger brothers and sisters. When your child is ready to move from the easy reader to a simple text Bible, try *God's Story*, a simplified Bible that puts the events and writings of the Bible in chronological order. It includes every book in the Bible and gives children the big picture of God working in our world. From *God's Story*, move your child into an understandable, full-text, traditionally-ordered Bible. And teach him how to find his way to the different books in the Bible.

God is sovereign

GOD is Lord. That means he's the boss. He's in charge. He knows what's best for us.

86. Can I Fill Myself?

HOLD a paper cup in one hand. What was a cup made for? To fulfill its purpose, to be all it was meant to be, it must be filled with something. Let's say you are thirsty. You want to drink from this cup. So you start to pour some water into it. But it closes off its opening. (Pinch the top of the cup closed.) It says, "No. I can fill myself." Can it fill itself? No. It has to depend on us to fill it. Neither can we fill ourselves with the gifts God wants us to have so we can be what we should be. We have to depend on God.

WHAT if you want to fill the cup with water but it closes its top and says, "No. I don't want water. I want buttermilk." But you say, "I don't want to drink buttermilk.

I want to drink water." Will the cup please you if it's filled with buttermilk? No.

Not if you want water. In the same way, we rely on God to make us into the

person he wants us to be. Sometimes we may wish God had made us differently.

But to fulfill the purpose for which God made each of us, we have to let him fill us

as he wants.

87. The Weaving

SHOW your children the underside of a weaving, tapestry, rug, or sweater in which the pattern is clear on the front but unclear on the back.

Life is like a weaving in which we see only the underside. Sometimes we don't understand what is happening. But God is like a weaver who has the whole beautiful pattern in mind. He knows exactly what he is doing in our lives for our good and his glory. It may look like a mess to us, but God is in control. If we continue to love and trust him, he will make our life turn out to be good and beautiful. Our life will be like the pattern we see on the top of something that has been woven.

88. Letting Jesus Drive

WHEN you prepare for a long trip by car, let your children look at maps with you. Talk about your itinerary. In our lives, there is no map. We don't know what is ahead. But God does. He has a master plan of what he is doing in the world, and he knows just where we fit in. He has a purpose and plan for each person. Identify the people in your family who can take turns driving. Who can drive, and who can't? Why? Asking Jesus to be our Lord means asking him to be in charge, to "drive" our lives. Jesus knows where to go and how fast to go. So we trust him and go with him.

89. The Puzzle

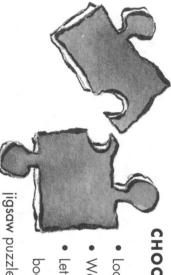

CHOOSE one of the following activities:

- Look at a few jigsaw puzzle pieces.
- Work a jigsaw puzzle with your family.
- Let each person draw a picture on cardboard and cut it into fairly large jigsaw puzzle pieces. Each person gives his puzzle to another person, and everyone works the puzzle he was given.

HOLD one puzzle piece in your hand. Tell your children that we are like a puzzle piece in God's hand. We can't see the big picture of life that God sees.

He is working out his great plan. Sometimes we don't know where we fit in God's plan. But as long as we are in God's hand, loving and trusting him, he will place us where he wants us. God links us with others in his kingdom to accomplish his purposes.

God cares

DAVID was awed by the fact that the great Creator of the universe cared about people. He wrote, "When I consider your heavens, the work of your fingers, the moon and the stars, which you have set in place, what is man that you are mindful of him, the son of man that you care for him?" (Psalm 8:3-4). Yet God does care passionately about each of us. His protection, his provision, and his presence in our lives demonstrate his care.

90. Our Fortress

VISIT a fort or look at pictures of forts. Then build a fort with blocks, building toys, or even pillows. Read 2 Samuel 22:2; Psalm 18:2; and Psalm 46:7. A fortress is a fort. How is God like a fort for us? God cares for us. He protects us.

91. A Shield

HELP your children make large shields out of cardboard or poster board. They can use markers or crayons to color designs on the shields, or they can cover the shields with aluminum foil. Tell them that the Bible says God is our shield. Ask your children what they think that means. What did a shield do for soldiers? What does a windshield do for us? How does a bulletproof vest shield a police officer? Read some Scriptures that call God our shield. Here are a few: Genesis 15:1; Deuteronomy 33:29; 2 Samuel 22:3, 31; Psalm 3:3; 7:10. God cares about us when we have trouble.

92. Loving the Needy

JOIN a ministry of outreach to the poor. It can be one that's sponsored by your church, or it might be sponsored by an organization in your community or city. Volunteer as a family to help feed the homeless or gather clothes and other goods for victims of natural disasters. Pray for the poor and needy. If possible, go on a short-term mission trip to a poor area. Demonstrating God's love for the needy (see Psalm 82:3-4) is more powerful than talking about God's love.

93. Listen

LISTEN to your children's feelings when they talk to you. Then choose a Bible story that tells about someone who may have felt the same way. Tell or read this story to them at a time when you can let them know that God cares about their feelings.

94. Torn-Paper Picture

GIVE each of your children a piece of plain paper, any color. Take another piece of paper, a different color, and tear it into several smaller pieces of random shapes. Give one piece to each child. Ask your children to look at their pieces and think of an object or animal that their piece reminds them of. Then have them glue the torn paper to the first piece of paper. Encourage them to draw a picture that incorporates the torn paper as part of the object or animal they imagined it to be. Talk about how our lives sometimes seem to be like that torn piece of paper. We feel weird or different or useless. But God cares. He sees the beauty in us and knows exactly where we fit into his big picture. And no matter how torn up our lives may seem, "In all things God works for the good of those who love him" (Romans 8:28).

95. Chosen

DO one of the following:

- Stir up something yummy to eat in the kitchen and ask, "Who wants to lick the spoon?"

- Play "Hide and Seek" and ask, "Who wants to be it?"

- As you head for your car with your family ask, "Who wants to sit in the front seat?"

THEN as your children lick the spoon, ride in the car, or stop playing "Hide and Seek," ask them to tell you about other times when they have wanted to be chosen. Did they want to be chosen for a certain team in gym class, for a part in a play, or for the group that raises the flag at school? Tell your children that God has chosen them to be part of his family. God loves each one of them. He knows each one of them. He cares about each one of them.

God satisfies us

GOD is the only one who can give us a feeling of being perfectly content and satisfied forever. He gives us everlasting joy and peace.

96. The Paper Cross

TELL this story using a piece of plain white paper.

THERE was once a wealthy man who had everything he could want. But he also had something he didn't want. He had an empty feeling inside. So he thought about what could make him happy. He decided that if he bought a sailboat, he'd be happy.

Fold one of the top corners down, making a diagonal fold that looks like a sail. (The top of the page should line up with one side of the page.) So he bought a boat and went sailing. And he was really happy. For a little while. The empty feeling came back. He thought and thought and finally decided that if he had a new house, he'd be happy.

Fold the other top corner down to make a pointed roof. So he bought a new house. It was on a hillside. He could watch the sun set from his window. And he was really happy. For a little while. The empty feeling came back. He thought, "Staying at home is not good for me. I need to travel." So he bought an airplane.

Fold the figure in half vertically, turn it so that the fold is at the bottom, and fold down the top sections to make wings. He flew all around the world and saw so many wonderful things! He was really happy! For a little while. The empty feeling came back. He thought, "Flying around is for the birds. I need to do something unique. Something most people never get to do. I'll take a rocket ship into space!"

Tear the wings off the airplane and open the center fold so that it looks like a rocket ship. So he took a rocket ship into outer space and saw the world very small below. He was very happy. For a while. The empty feeling came back. He looked and looked, and he finally found that there was only one thing that would make him happy.

Unfold the figure to see a cross. And how long did it last? Forever!

(Adapted from an unknown source)

97. Hunger and Thirst

SOMETIME when your child is hungry or thirsty, ask her to describe what it feels like to be hungry or thirsty. Read Psalm 42:1-2. Ask if your child has ever felt thirsty or hungry for God. If so, ask what it feels like. If not, describe what it feels like for you. Read these verses: Deuteronomy 4:27-29; Jeremiah 29:13; Matthew 5:6; 7:7.

98. Empty Heart, Full Heart

WITH a three-by-five index card held horizontally, draw a line down the center of the card from top to bottom. To the immediate left of the center line, draw a large heart. To the immediate right of the line, draw a cross. Ask your child to hold the card in front of him at arm's length and slowly pull it toward his eyes while staring at the center of the line. As the card gets closer to your child's eyes, the cross will appear to move into the center of the heart. Talk about the kinds of things people use to fill their empty lives. Nothing will fulfill us like Jesus.

99. What Will Satisfy?

GET a magazine that is suitable for everyone in your family to see. Go through the magazine with your children, letting them point out pictures of the types of things that people do and buy in an effort to find something that will satisfy them or make them happy. Do these things last? Can these things satisfy people? Jesus is the only one who can satisfy us forever.

100. My Portion

BAKE or buy a pie or pizza. Cut it into wedges and serve a wedge to each person in your family. Tell each one, "This is your portion." While everyone is eating, read Psalm 73:26: "God is the strength of my heart and my portion forever." Talk about how a portion of pie or pizza is only a part.

If each person gets only one piece, you may still be hungry for more. But God is so great that in life, if God is your portion, you have everything you need. "His divine power has given us everything we need for life and godliness" (2 Peter 1:3). Ask your children to talk about some of the things God has given your family. Include spiritual as well as physical gifts and blessings.

about the author

KARYN HENLEY is an award-winning author, educator, and children's performer. Her original version of *The Beginner's Bible*, which was born out of a deep passion to make the Bible understandable to young children, has sold over 3 million copies. In addition to that Bible and her wide range of products for Tyndale House, Karyn has produced numerous resources for parents, teachers, and children. These include *My First Hymnal*, the Creative Bible Learning series, and *Tails* storybooks.

Based on her book *Child Sensitive Teaching*, Karyn has presented seminars to parents and teachers in North America as well as Australia, New Zealand, Russia, East Africa, and England. Her PLAYSONGS Concerts, during which she presents her delightful original music and skits that teach children about praise and worship, are also in great demand.

Karyn was born in Austin, Texas, and grew up in Abilene. She began teaching at the age of 14 when her mother, a Sunday school supervisor, asked her to be the teacher for a class of 18-month-olds. Karyn has been working with children ever since! She studied elementary education at Abilene Christian University, earning a bachelor's degree with a certification to teach kindergarten. Now she has over 30 years of experience in the classroom.

It is Karyn's desire to help teachers and parents understand the principles of communicating with children and how to apply those principles with confidence and compassion. She is an avid reader and writer, working many hours a week to keep her seminars and material abreast of the latest research in child psychology and spiritual development.

Karyn lives in Nashville, Tennessee, with her husband Ralph, their two sons, Ray and Heath, and their two cats, Nip and Tuck.

For a schedule of upcoming seminars and concerts, visit Karyn's Web site at www.KarynHenley.com

If you liked

100 Ways to Teach Your Child about God,
check out these other Karyn Henley products:

God's Story bridges the gap between Bible storybooks and full-text Bibles with over 800 stories specifically targeted to early readers. Also includes a 14 page timeline and helpful lists. For ages 4-8.

0-8423-0743-5

God's Story and Me This companion to God's Story offers 52 full-week devotionals on great topics kids ages 4-8 will love to talk about.

0-8423-4361-X

Sword Fighting teaches kids how to use the Bible to make important decisions. School-aged kids will have fun with this 365 day devotional as they examine biblical examples, memorize verses, and use this knowledge for friendly sword-fighting application games.
0-8423-3465-3

Before I Dream series: Let Karyn Henley tell your child a bedtime Bible story, then sing him a gentle song as he drifts off to sleep. In this new audio Bible story format, beautiful instrumental music underscores Karyn's soothing storytelling style, and each story is followed by an original song that focuses on the story's theme.

Dream of Heaven includes stories about Creation, Moses, Jesus stilling the storm, the lost sheep, Peter escaping from prison, and John's vision into heaven.
0-8423-3448-3

Lord, I Love You includes stories about the Lord's Prayer, Mary anointing Jesus, Daniel in the lions' den, Esther, Samuel, and God's pillar of fire.
0-8423-3471-8

In Jesus' Arms includes stories about Noah and the ark, Jesus and the children, the Sermon on the Mount, Jesus' birth, Joseph, and David.
0-8423-3473-4

PLAYSONGS™ audio/video line: These Playsongs live action videos and audio cassettes/CDs help your preschoolers develop a good foundation for a lifelong relationship with Jesus. Each audio features music and storytelling. *Kitchen Band Parade* focuses on expressing thankfulness and worship to God. *I Feel Like a Giggle* reminds kids that God loves and cares for them. The joys of God's wonderful world are explored in *Five Little Ladybugs*. The companion videos show Karyn "in her element" with young children, music, bright colorful settings, fun costumes, and props.

I Feel Like a Giggle

CD 0-8423-3459-9

Cassette 0-8423-3441-6

Video 0-8423-3445-9

Five Little Ladybugs

CD 0-8423-3458-0

Cassette 0-8423-3440-8

Video 0-8423-3444-0

Kitchen Band Parade

CD 0-8423-3457-2

Cassette 0-8423-3439-4

Video 0-8423-3443-2

PLAYSONGS™ books: A fun addition to the other Playsongs products!

Five Little Ladybugs helps children have fun while they learn to count.
0-8423-3469-6

In ***L-O-V-E***, children learn about God's love for them.
0-8423-3468-8

In the bedtime fun book ***Noah's Zoo***, children help Noah put the animals to bed.
0-8423-3466-1